LIVING WITH DISEASES AND DISORDERS
Migraines and Seizures

LIVING WITH DISEASES AND DISORDERS

Migraines and Seizures

REBECCA SHERMAN

SERIES ADVISOR

HEATHER L. PELLETIER, Ph.D.

Pediatric Psychologist, Hasbro Children's Hospital

Clinical Assistant Professor, Warren Alpert Medical School of Brown University

MASON CREST

Mason Crest
450 Parkway Drive, Suite D
Broomall, PA 19008
www.masoncrest.com

MTM Publishing, Inc.
435 West 23rd Street, #8C
New York, NY 10011
www.mtmpublishing.com

President: Valerie Tomaselli
Vice President, Book Development: Hilary Poole
Designer: Annemarie Redmond
Copyeditor: Peter Jaskowiak
Editorial Assistant: Leigh Eron

Series ISBN: 978-1-4222-3747-2
Hardback ISBN: 978-1-4222-3757-1
E-Book ISBN: 978-1-4222-8038-6

Library of Congress Cataloging-in-Publication Data
Names: Sherman, Rebecca, author.
Title: Migraines and seizures / by Rebecca Sherman; series consultant, Heather Pelletier, PhD, Hasbro Children's Hospital, Alpert Medical School/Brown University.
Description: Broomall, PA: Mason Crest, [2018] | Series: Living with diseases and disorders | Audience: Age: 12+ | Audience: Grade 7 to 8. | Includes index.
Identifiers: LCCN 2017000401| ISBN 9781422237571 (hardback: alk. paper) | ISBN 9781422280386 (ebook)
Subjects: LCSH: Migraine—Juvenile literature. | Epilepsy—Juvenile literature.
Classification: LCC RC392 .S486 2018 | DDC 616.8/4912—dc23
LC record available at https://lccn.loc.gov/2017000401

Printed and bound in the United States of America.

First printing
9 8 7 6 5 4 3 2 1

TABLE OF CONTENTS

Key Icons to Look for:

 Words to Understand: These words with their easy-to-understand definitions will increase the reader's understanding of the text, while building vocabulary skills.

 Sidebars: This boxed material within the main text allows readers to build knowledge, gain insights, explore possibilities, and broaden their perspectives by weaving together additional information to provide realistic and holistic perspectives.

 Educational Videos: Readers can view videos by scanning our QR codes, which will provide them with additional educational content to supplement the text. Examples include news coverage, moments in history, speeches, iconic sports moments, and much more.

 Text-Dependent Questions: These questions send the reader back to the text for more careful attention to the evidence presented there.

 Research Projects: Readers are pointed toward areas of further inquiry connected to each chapter. Suggestions are provided for projects that encourage deeper research and analysis.

 Series Glossary of Key Terms: This back-of-the-book glossary contains terminology used throughout the series. Words found here increase the reader's ability to read and comprehend higher-level books and articles in this field.

SERIES INTRODUCTION

According to the Chronic Disease Center at the Centers for Disease Control and Prevention, over 100 million Americans suffer from a chronic illness or medical condition. In other words, they have a health problem that lasts three months or more, affects their ability to perform normal activities, and requires frequent medical care and/or hospitalizations. Epidemiological studies suggest that between 15 and 18 million of those with chronic illness or medical conditions are children and adolescents. That's roughly one out of every four children in the United States.

These young people must exert more time and energy to complete the tasks their peers do with minimal thought. For example, kids with Crohn's disease, ulcerative colitis, or other digestive issues have to plan meals and snacks carefully, to make sure they are not eating food that could irritate their stomachs or cause pain and discomfort. People with cerebral palsy, muscular dystrophy, or other physical limitations associated with a medical condition may need help getting dressed, using the bathroom, or joining an activity in gym class. Those with cystic fibrosis, asthma, or epilepsy may have to avoid certain activities or environments altogether. ADHD and other behavior disorders require the individual to work harder to sustain the level of attention and focus necessary to keep up in school.

Living with a chronic illness or medical condition is not easy. Identifying a diagnosis and adjusting to the initial shock is only the beginning of a long journey. Medications, follow-up appointments and procedures, missed school or work, adjusting to treatment regimens, coping with uncertainty, and readjusting expectations are all hurdles one has to overcome in learning how to live one's best life. Naturally, feelings of sadness or anxiety may set in while learning how to make it all work. This is especially true for young people, who may reach a point in their medical journey when they have to rethink some of their original goals and life plans to better match their health reality.

Chances are, you know people who live this reality on a regular basis. It is important to remember that those affected by chronic illness are family members, neighbors, friends, or maybe even our own doctors. They are likely navigating the demands of the day a little differently, as they balance the specific accommodations necessary to manage their illness. But they have the same desire to be productive and included as those who are fortunate not to have a chronic illness.

This set provides valuable information about the most common childhood chronic illnesses, in language that is engaging and easy for students to grasp. Each chapter highlights important vocabulary words and offers text-dependent questions to help assess comprehension. Meanwhile, educational videos (available by scanning QR codes) and research projects help connect the text to the outside world.

Our mission with this set is twofold. First, the volumes provide a go-to source for information about chronic illness for young people who are living with particular conditions. Each volume in this set strives to provide reliable medical information and practical advice for living day-to-day with various challenges. Second, we hope these volumes will also help kids without chronic illness better understand and appreciate how people with health challenges live. After all, if one in four young people is managing a health condition, it's safe to assume that the majority of our youth already know someone with a chronic illness, whether they realize it or not.

With the growing presence of social media, bullying is easier than ever before. It's vital that young people take a moment to stop and think about how they are more similar to kids with health challenges than they are different. Poor understanding and low tolerance for individual differences are often the platforms for bullying and noninclusive behavior, both in person and online. Living with Diseases and Disorders strives to close the gap of misunderstanding.

The ultimate solution to the bullying problem is surely an increase in empathy. We hope these books will help readers better understand and appreciate not only the daily struggles of people living with chronic conditions, but their triumphs as well.

—Heather Pelletier, Ph.D.
Hasbro Children's Hospital
Warren Alpert Medical School of Brown University

WORDS TO UNDERSTAND

axons: thin fibers that extend from the cell bodies of neurons to carry messages.

cerebellum: the back part of the brain; it controls movement.

cerebrum: the front part of the brain; it controls many higher-level thinking functions.

dendrite: branch-like extension of a neuron that receives signals from other cells.

depolarize: to reduce or remove a magnetic charge.

electrochemical: interactions between molecules involving their electrical and chemical properties.

ganglia: plural of ganglion; a cluster of nerve cells and part of the peripheral nervous system.

ion: an atom or molecule that has lost or gained electrons, giving it a negative or positive charge.

millivolt: a measure of electric current equaling one thousandth of a volt.

nerves: bundles of axons that communicate with cells all around the body.

neurons: special cells in the nervous system designed to transmit messages.

neurotransmitters: chemicals used by neurons to communicate.

synapse: a tiny gap across which neurons communicate using neurotransmitters.

vesicles: tiny blisters or sacs filled with fluid.

CHAPTER ONE

The Brain and Nervous System

Walking. Talking. Sleeping. Seeing. Thinking. All of these activities are controlled by the most amazing structure in the human body: the nervous system. Run by your brain, your nervous system makes you the unique person you are. It connects you to the world through your senses. Your brain collects all the information you gather by seeing, hearing, touching, smelling, tasting, and moving. But it doesn't just store that information, like a computer's hard drive might. Your brain learns from everything you do and experience.

Your brain can make decisions in a split second. If you touch something too hot on the stove, your brain immediately sends a message along the spinal cord, telling your muscles to pull your hand back, and it makes a memory of the experience so that you'll know to be careful around the stove next time. Your brain can also make decisions based on evidence accumulated over a long period of time. If your dad makes a joke at dinner, your brain tells you to laugh—or groan—depending on how many times he's already told that joke and how funny it was the first time.

Hot stoves are dangerous, and usually our brains won't let us make the mistake of touching one more than once.

When something goes wrong with the nervous system, it can have a profound effect on everything that makes you who you are. Neurology is the study of the brain and the nervous system. Problems with the nervous system are called *neurological disorders*. A neurologist is a type of doctor who specializes in treating neurological disorders, of which there are many, many types. Some are very serious, and even life-threatening. Others aren't life-threatening but they do make life more challenging.

Some neurological disorders generally affect older people and the elderly. Some affect infants, kids, teens, or people of any age. Seizures and migraines are two neurological disorders that can affect people of any age. To understand the impact that seizures, migraines, and other neurological disorders can have, first let's take a closer look at how the nervous system works.

The Nervous System

The nervous system is divided into two parts. The central nervous system (CNS) is the command center. Made up of the brain and the spinal cord that runs down your back, the central nervous system is the boss of you. But, like any boss, it

Nervous System

central nervous system

brain

spinal cord

peripheral
nervous system

ganglia

nerves

central nervous system

brain

spinal cord

peripheral
nervous system

ganglia

nerves

The human nervous system in a woman (left) and man (right).

BRAIN SCANS AND IMAGING

How can doctors see what's going on inside your head? There are a few different methods available:

- **Electroencephalogram (EEG).** This painless test monitors electrical activity in your brain using small metal disks pasted to your scalp. These electrodes record the electrical pulses taking place in your brain. They send those records via wires to a computer, which plots your brain waves as a graph. Your doctor is specially trained to analyze that graph in order to spot abnormal electrical surges that might indicate epileptic seizures. EEGs are often combined with video monitoring, so your doctor can match movements you make to the brain waves that caused them. You can have an EEG when you're asleep or awake.

- **Magnetic resonance imagery (MRI).** For an MRI, you lie down in an enclosed tube, where strong magnetic fields and radio waves are used to make computerized images of your brain and your blood vessels. The images reveal areas where tissue is injured or abnormal. During an MRI, you may be asked to lie completely still. Or a doctor may ask you to perform certain tasks in order to see how a certain region of your brain is working.

- **Computed tomography scan (CT scan).** This test combines X-rays with computer imaging to look at horizontal slices of the brain in tremendous detail. Both CT scans (sometimes called CAT scans) and MRIs may require the use of contrast dye. This is usually injected into the patient before the test in order to make images more clear.

can't do its job without help. That's where the peripheral nervous system (PNS) comes in. The PNS gathers data from the senses and from all over the body via your **nerves** and **ganglia**. It sends that data to the CNS. The CNS decides how to respond, and sends messages back to the PNS directing the body to take one or more actions.

If you're walking in the woods and see a bear, your nervous system sends data from your eyes to your brain. Your brain processes that information and sends back immediate responses. It may direct your leg muscles to run away as fast as you can. The PNS makes those leg muscles move. But the brain is the part that recognizes a bear and decides that you are in danger.

The Great Brain

The brain sits at the top and back of your head, protected by your hair, the skin of your scalp, and your bony skull. Inside the skull, the brain is further protected by three layers of membranes called the *meninges*. Squeezed into this protected space, the brain contains an estimated 100 billion special cells called **neurons**. Neurons communicate with one another via pathways throughout the brain. They communicate with other types of cells throughout the body via the spinal cord and the peripheral nervous system. Neurons are not the only type of cells in the brain, but the work they do is what puts the brain in charge.

The brain is organized into three different sections: the forebrain, the midbrain, and the hindbrain. The hindbrain manages physical activities that you do without thinking; it makes your heart beat regularly, for example, and your lungs breathe in and out. The hindbrain also contains the **cerebellum**, which manages some types of movement. If you hit a baseball for a home run—or swing and miss for the out—your cerebellum was calling the shots.

Located deep inside the brain, the midbrain is responsible for routing messages to and from the brain to the rest of the body via the spinal cord.

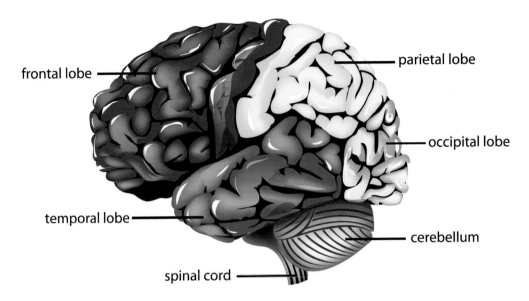

The main parts of the human brain.

The **cerebrum**, in the forebrain, is by far the largest and most complex part of the brain. It is divided into two sides, the right and left hemispheres. The left hemisphere controls the right side of your body, and the right hemisphere controls the left side of your body. The two sides look similar, but they are not identical, and they do not necessarily serve the same functions. Both the cerebrum and the cerebellum are covered by the cerebral cortex, commonly known as "gray matter."

Besides its two hemispheres, the cerebrum is further divided into four lobes. The frontal lobes control your voluntary actions—the things you do on purpose, like walking around or picking up an object. They also help you consider different ideas, and decide how to behave in a situation. Behind the frontal lobes, the parietal lobes collect and process the data you pick up from your senses, including your sense of the space around you. They also help you read and do math. The occipital lobes manage and remember information coming from your eyes, while the temporal lobes do the same for the information coming from your ears.

NEUROTRANSMITTERS AND SYNAPSES

To send an electrical signal from one neuron to another, the axon terminal of the neuron must touch the neuron it's trying to reach. But there is another way for neurons to communicate with each other even when there is a gap between them. To do so, an axon terminal translates an electrically charged signal into a chemical signal.

When the electrical signal arrives, the axon terminal activates synaptic **vesicles** filled with tiny amounts of certain chemicals called neurotransmitters. These vesicles open, releasing their contents into the gap between the cells. This gap is called the synapse. The neurotransmitters travel across this gap to receptors in the dendrites of another neuron. The neurotransmitters received by this neuron act as a stimulus, causing the neuron to open ion channels and pass the message along in the form of an electrical charge. The process repeats, traveling from neuron to neuron, until the message arrives at its final destination. But if something keeps the process from working properly, it can cause a variety of brain disorders, including epilepsy.

Many thought processes and bodily functions are affected by more than one area of the brain. But damage to an area of the brain can affect or even destroy a person's ability to use any function managed by that area. For instance, your eyes might work just fine, but if your occipital lobes are damaged, you may become blind. That's because the information that your eyes receive can't be communicated anymore. It's as though you took a photo with your phone to post online, but then you couldn't connect to the Internet. Your eyes need your neurons to make the connection.

A Closer Look at Neurons

Neurons are unique. They have a cell body, which contains many of the same structures as are found in other types of cells. But they also have two types of

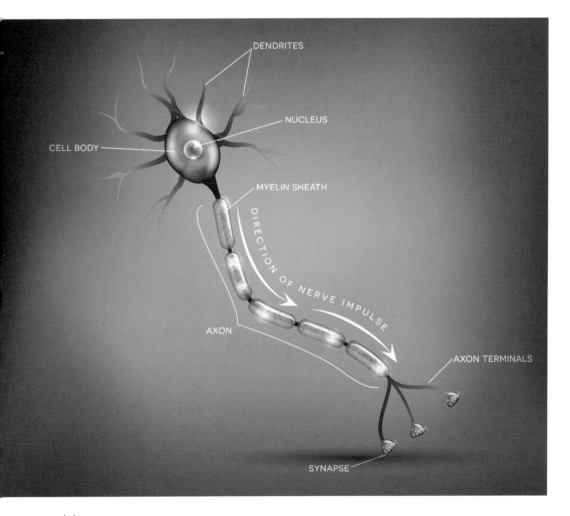

A human neuron.

structures extending from the cell body that are found in no other types of cell. These two structures are how neurons communicate with one another, and with other types of cells.

Axons are long, thin extensions that project out from neurons. Generally, each neuron has one axon, but that axon can stretch a surprising distance— some are up to 3 feet long! Axons send messages from neurons using tiny amounts of electricity. But you've never plugged in your axons. Where do they get this electricity? By manipulating the flow of electrically charged atoms called **ions**, axons create electrical charges that travel down their length like a power line.

EDUCATIONAL VIDEO

Scan this code to watch a video about the nervous system.

Neurons use another special extension to receive messages. This extension is called a **dendrite**. A single neuron can have many dendrites, and each dendrite can have many branches, like a tree. The point of contact at which a dendrite receives messages from an axon is called a **synapse**. Some neurons can receive electrical signals directly, but many neurons receive messages in the form of **electrochemical** signals called **neurotransmitters**. These are tiny molecules that are released by the end of the axon when it receives an electrical signal. The dendrite absorbs these neurotransmitter molecules, and, in doing so, receives the message sent. This electrochemical signaling is the basis for all of your brain activity.

When you're learning, your synapses are very busy transmitting messages from one neuron to another. By learning new things, you cause your neurons to make new connections. The more you learn, the more connections you make.

ACTION POTENTIAL

When they are not transmitting messages, axons have a very slight negative electrical charge of about 70 **millivolts** (mV). A negative charge attracts positively charged ions, just like positive and negative magnets attract one another. Positively charged ions gather around axons. But axons have a protective membrane that only allows ions to enter at special gated passages, called *ion channels*. These channels are kept closed until an axon receives a stimulus telling it to send a message.

Then the axon opens the ion channels to admit positively charged ions. These rush into the axon, **depolarizing** it. This causes the axon to send an action potential, also called a nerve impulse, down its length to its terminal, or end. At the axon terminal, the message is relayed to another neuron or cell. Once the message has been sent, the axon stops admitting positively charged ions. Instead, it expels positively charged ions using a complex system of ion channels and pumps until it reaches its original negative resting charge.

The entire process takes about a thousandth of a second, so an axon can send up to 300 messages per second. Neurons can get overexcited and send messages too frequently. Or they may be underexcited and not send messages frequently enough. Either issue can disrupt regular brain function.

When you make the effort to learn something really well, those connections get more established. That's why practicing a new skill is the key to getting better at it. But with so much happening in your brain all the time, things can sometimes go wrong. The processes that neurons use to send messages to one another can be interrupted, disrupted, or damaged. This can make it harder for you to learn or think clearly. It can also affect your body's ability to perform basic tasks, and it can cause headaches or seizures.

Problems in the brain can be temporary. For example, some problems are caused by stress, emotional upset, poor nutrition, too little sleep, an injury, or an infection. Sometimes they are caused by more serious, chronic problems stemming from genetic mutations that make it harder for neurons or other cells to do their jobs. Serious injuries and infections may also cause scarring in brain tissue, causing permanent problems. Some common neurological disorders, like epilepsy or migraines, can have more than one cause. Sometimes doctors cannot determine the cause of seizures or migraines, but they may still be able to offer treatment for symptoms.

Text-Dependent Questions

1. What is the study of the nervous system called? Who are the doctors who study it?
2. What are the parts of the nervous system? Which part is in charge?
3. Describe how a neuron is different from other types of cells.

Research Project

To learn more about how your nervous system generates electricity and uses it to send messages, try watching this Crash Course video: www.youtube.com/watch?v=OZG8M_ldA1M. After you watch, make a list of the steps involved.

WORDS TO UNDERSTAND

aura: an odd sense of warning before a seizure or migraine.

automatisms: repetitive actions performed automatically or unwillingly during a seizure.

biofeedback: a technique used to teach someone how to control some bodily functions.

constrict: make narrower.

deja vu: an odd sense of having experienced something before.

epilepsy: any of the syndromes or conditions that cause epileptic seizures.

epileptic seizure: a storm of abnormal electrochemical signaling in the brain.

febrile seizures: seizures caused by high fevers.

focus: in a seizure, a particular part of the brain where abnormal signaling occurs.

postictal state: the condition of recovering after a seizure.

prodomes: symptoms that appear before an attack of illness.

refractory: stubborn, difficult to treat.

resection: surgically cutting out a piece of a bodily organ.

trigger: something that causes something else to happen.

vagus nerve: a nerve extending from the brain stem to several organs in the chest and abdomen.

CHAPTER TWO

Understanding Seizures and Migraines

A bolt of lightning carries tremendous electrical energy. It can hit power lines or transmission towers, frying circuits and knocking out electricity. Appliances and devices connected to the grid may go dark and lose data. Depending on where the lightning struck, the damage may be confined to a single house or neighborhood. Sometimes, though rarely, an entire city or region may go dark.

Something like the effects of a lightning strike can occur on a very tiny scale in the human brain. You remember that the brain creates its own electricity so that neurons can use it to communicate. An electrochemical storm inside the brain strikes at the network of neurons that send messages back and forth. These storms may occur because some portion of the signaling system isn't working properly. Injuries or genetic mutations can change how well any single element works. One mutation may affect the functioning of certain ion channels. Another may change how sensitive synapses are.

One portion of the network may be affected, like a single lobe on one side

A seizure is a bit like an electrical storm inside the brain.

of the brain. Or the entire network—the whole brain—may be hit by the storm. If lightning strikes your community's power and data grids, your refrigerator and TV may stop working, and any unsaved progress on your gaming console or computer may be lost. If a storm hits your brain, some of your functions may stop working, like walking, talking, and being aware of what's around you. Some data may be lost, too. If the storm is very severe, or if it goes on for too long a time, the brain's network may be permanently damaged.

These kinds of electrochemical storms are called **epileptic seizures**. And a person who has two or more epileptic seizures has a condition called **epilepsy**. During a seizure, clusters of neurons send messages at abnormal rates. They send messages too rapidly, or too many neurons send messages all at once. Like a web page that stops being able to load if too many people try to access it at the same time, a seizure overloads the brain's ability to function properly.

An overloaded computer might freeze up, flash the same screen over and over, or shut down altogether. A person having a seizure may freeze up, flail around, or fall down and lose consciousness. There may not be any visible symptoms at all, but instead the person may have odd sensations or feelings. There are many different types of epileptic seizures. They are defined by the effect they have on the person having the seizure.

There are two categories of epileptic seizures: *focal seizures* and *generalized seizures*. Focal seizures are the more common category, affecting some 60 percent of people with epilepsy. A focal seizure causes abnormal electrical signaling in one limited portion of the brain, known as the **focus**. A generalized seizure may start as a focus, but then spread rapidly to encompass both hemispheres of the brain.

Focal Seizures

There are a few different types of focal seizures, described by the area of the brain in which they occur. For example, a *focal frontal lobe seizure* takes place in one of the brain's frontal lobes.

SEIZURE TREATMENTS: MEDICATION

Medication is the first line of defense against seizures. There are tens of different anti-seizure medication. They each have different recommended uses. They can also have some side effects. Your doctor will try to adjust how much medication you take so that you get the most effective seizure control with the fewest side effects.

When choosing medication, your doctor will consider the kind of seizures you've had, as well as what may have caused those seizures. In some cases, you may be asked to try different medications. Some people need to take more than one medication to control seizures. But roughly 7 out of 10 people are successfully treated with medication. These individuals have few or no seizures thanks to treatment. Seizures that continue without improvement despite medication are called **refractory** seizures.

Even if you've had no seizures for a long time, it is really important to continue taking your medication as directed. Skipping a dose or stopping altogether can trigger severe seizures.

Focal seizures generally last no more than a minute or two. People having a focal seizure may suddenly have a weird feeling of happiness, anger, sadness, or even nausea. They may suddenly hear, see, taste, or smell something that isn't really there. They may have a sense of **deja vu**, in which they feel like they've already experienced what is happening. Or the opposite may occur—they may feel that a familiar place or situation is completely unknown or foreign to them.

They may also move one part of their body, like a hand or a leg, in an odd, repetitive, automatic kind of way. These repetitive behaviors are called **automatisms**, and they can involve more complicated actions, too. A person might walk around in a tight circle, or wash the same dish over and over again. All of these movements are involuntary, meaning they cannot be controlled by the person having the seizure.

In simple partial seizures, people retain awareness of what is happening during the seizure. In complex partial seizures, they remains conscious—that is, they still appear to be awake. But they do not have any awareness of what is happening and will not remember the seizure afterwards.

Generalized Seizures

In a generalized seizure, the storm of abnormal signaling seizes control of both sides of the brain. Generalized seizures can cause a person to lose consciousness, or to fall suddenly. They can cause a person's muscles to jerk violently back and forth in movements called convulsions. These sudden falls and convulsions are what many people think of when they think of epilepsy and seizures. But these are not the whole story. There are many different types of generalized seizures.

- **Absence seizures.** Once called *petit mal seizures*, these are common among kids age 4–14. They may look like a person staring silently off into space, as though he or she has been distracted by a daydream.

EDUCATIONAL VIDEO

Scan this code to watch a video about seizures.

Unlike a daydreamer, someone having an absence seizure will have no memory or awareness of what is going on, even if someone, like a teacher, tries to get their attention. Simple absence seizures may last for only a few seconds. In fact, they happen so quickly that sometimes no one even notices they occurred. They may occur so frequently that a person has more than one hundred of them over the course of a single day. This can make it difficult or even impossible for a kid to pay attention or learn in school. In complex absence seizures, the person may have a slight twitch. He may blink or move his mouth or hands repetitively.

- **Myoclonic seizures.** These cause the person having a seizure to suddenly jerk or twitch, generally in the head, neck, shoulders, or arms. These seizures usually happen one at a time, but they can occur in clusters, with each seizure lasting a second or two. The person may suddenly seem very clumsy, dropping whatever is in her or his hands.

- **Atonic seizures.** A kid having an atonic seizure suddenly loses muscle tone. These seizures cause the eyelids and head to droop. Someone standing when the seizure hits will slump or fall to the ground, and may be injured by the fall.

- **Tonic seizures.** The opposite of atonic seizures, these cause a person's muscles to suddenly become rigid, or locked into place. A person standing during a tonic seizure may fall to the ground stiffly, like a tree. Again, these may cause injuries.

- **Tonic-clonic seizures.** These are the falling, convulsive seizures that most people associate with epilepsy. If you're watching a person have a tonic-clonic seizure, you may see her suddenly cry out. Then you will see her lose consciousness, fall like a tree, and then begin jerking violently. Once called *grand mal seizures,* they can cause a person to bite his or her tongue, or lose bowel and bladder control. These seizures usually last 1–3 minutes. If they last more than 5 minutes, the person having the seizure requires immediate medical help.

SEIZURE TREATMENTS: DIET

For kids with severe, refractory seizures, a very restrictive diet called the *ketogenic diet* may offer hope. Usually the cells of the body get energy from nutrients in your food called carbohydrates. Bread, pasta, rice, fruit, and sweets are all filled with carbohydrates. If you don't eat enough carbohydrates, your body instead burns fats for energy. Fats are found in butter, lard, fatty meats, and oils, like olive oil and canola oil. When your body burns fats for energy, you produce chemical compounds called *ketones*. These ketones give the ketogenic diet its name. People on the diet have to strictly avoid food containing carbohydrates. They eat foods that are very high in fat.

The ketogenic diet has been in use since the 1920s. Scientists don't really understand why it reduces seizures. But study after study has proved that it really does reduce seizures, particularly for people with certain epileptic conditions.

A ketogenic diet cuts out as many carbohydrates as possible.

KETO Food Pyramid

Berries

Nuts and Seeds

Some Non Green Vegetables

Green Vegetables

Oils

Eggs and Dairy

Meat

NO:
Bread
Pasta
Sugar
Milk
Corn
Beans
Rice

SEIZURE TREATMENTS: SURGERY AND IMPLANTS

In cases when medications fail to control seizures, doctors may recommend brain surgery. Brain surgery is an option only under certain circumstances. Most commonly, doctors remove the focus, or area of the brain where the seizures originate. This kind of surgery is called a **resection**. If successful, it can cure a person of seizures. To successfully perform a resection, doctors must first pinpoint the focus of seizures.

Doctors can't remove an area of the brain if doing so would seriously disable the patient. If seizures occur in an area that can't be removed, doctors may instead surgically cut the networks or pathways through which seizures spread to other areas of the brain. This kind of disconnection procedure generally does not cure seizures, but it can make them less severe.

A device called a **vagus nerve** stimulator may be surgically implanted just under the skin in the chest. A wire connects the device to the vagus nerve in the neck. The device is programmed to send regular bursts of electricity to the vagus nerve. These bursts of electricity appear to make the brain less likely to have a seizure. More types of devices like this are under development.

Before and After a Seizure

Some people get a sort of warning, or premonition, before a seizure occurs. Called **auras** or **prodomes**, these warnings can be simply an odd feeling that something isn't right or that a seizure will occur. Some people have a weird feeling, like butterflies in their stomach. Others might smell something odd, or feel unusually sensitive to light. In some cases, the aura itself is a mild seizure.

During a seizure, a person may lose consciousness or suffer injuries. These affect how a person feels after the seizure is over, during what is known as the **postictal state**. People who have had a brief seizure with no loss of awareness may be able to immediately get back to what they were doing before the seizure hit. People who have longer seizures or lose consciousness may be confused or exhausted afterward. It can take several minutes, or quite a bit longer, to recover. If a person was injured while having a seizure, first aid or emergency medical care should be given immediately.

Other Types of Seizures

Some seizures are not caused by abnormal brain signaling and are not considered epileptic seizures. **Febrile seizures** are common among kids and very young children. They occur when a child is running a high fever. These can look like tonic-clonic seizures, and they can be scary to watch. But most children who get febrile seizures grow out of it by their fifth birthday.

Psychogenic non-epileptic seizures (PNES) may also look like tonic-clonic seizures, but close monitoring with a video camera and an EEG shows that no abnormal signaling activity is happening in the brain during such seizures. Doctors believe PNES is caused by stress and emotional upset. That's why PNES is referred to as a functional neurological disorder, a condition in which someone's emotions affect the body, making that person genuinely sick. People with PNES are not faking their seizures. But, while epileptic seizures are treated by a neurologist, treatment for PNES is usually with someone who specializes in mental health, like a psychiatrist, psychotherapist, or social worker. Therapy and stress-management techniques help up to 80 percent of kids and teenagers with PNES become seizure-free.

Migraines

Most everyone gets a headache once in a while. One out of every 20 kids suffers from an unusually painful type of headache called a migraine. Migraines cause intense, throbbing pain that may affect one or both sides of the head. Someone with a migraine may feel dizzy or nauseous. He or she may become photosensitive, which is a condition in which bright lights seem unbearable. A person suffering from a migraine may be unable to do anything except sleep until he or she feels better. A migraine can last anywhere from 30 minutes to 1 or 2 days.

Like epileptic seizures, migraines may be preceded by an aura. The person may see odd bright or colored lights, spots, or lines. A person who is about to have a migraine may smell peculiar odors or get blurry vision.

Doctors still have a lot to learn about the causes of migraines, but it is thought that they occur when the blood vessels to the brain constrict, causing less blood to flow to the brain. The brain attempts to compensate by instructing other blood vessels to dilate, or open wider, so that more blood can flow. This causes pain and inflammation.

Migraines are usually treated with painkillers like acetaminophen or ibuprofen. If the migraine is preceded by an aura, doctors recommend taking painkillers as soon as possible, so that they have a chance to start working before the migraine begins. Someone who suffers frequent migraines may be prescribed special medication to prevent the migraine from developing or make it less severe. Some doctors recommend teaching biofeedback

TRIGGERS

Things that can provoke a seizure or a migraine are known as **triggers**. Each person with seizures or migraines has a unique set of triggers, but many people with seizures or migraines share certain triggers.

Common triggers for seizures
- flashing lights
- dehydration
- skipping a meal
- stress
- not getting enough sleep
- certain hormones produced during a girl's menstrual cycle
- missing a dose of anti-seizure medication
- alcohol or drug use

Common triggers for migraines
- stress
- dehydration
- poor nutrition
- certain foods, like hot dogs, chocolate, and some types of cheese
- too much caffeine (in coffee, tea, soda, and chocolate)
- too much sleep or too little sleep
- the menstrual cycle
- changes in the weather

About 10 percent of American teens experience migraines.

techniques that allow people with migraines to calm themselves when they think a migraine might be starting.

It is common for migraine sufferers to experience anywhere from one to four migraines per month. Boys and girls get migraines at equal rates until puberty, after which three times more girls than boys experience them. This gender imbalance leads scientists to believe that hormones affect a person's susceptibility to migraines.

Other Types of Headaches

Not all headaches are migraines. Here are some other common types of headache:

- **Tension headaches.** The most common kind of headache, these are triggered by stress. They come on slowly. The pain may feel dull rather than sharp, like having something wrapped too tightly around your head. These kind of headaches don't involve auras, nausea, or visual disturbances. They usually respond pretty well to over-the-counter pain medication.

- **Cluster headaches.** These produce a sharp, stabbing pain bad enough to wake you out of a sound sleep. They usually don't last for more than a couple of hours, but they occur in groups. You might get five or more headaches over a short period of time, which could be a single day or several days. The pain may be on one side of the head, and it may be accompanied by a runny nose.

- **Persistent daily headaches.** These are usually migraines or tension headaches, but they occur every day. People sometimes develop daily headaches as a result of taking painkillers too often. It's thought that the body becomes dependent on the daily dose of painkillers, creating a cycle that only ends when the person stops taking painkillers for a week to 10 days.

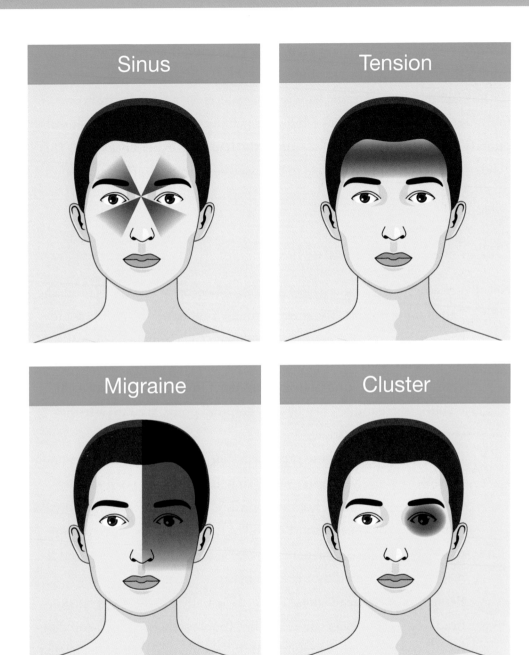

This diagram shows the general location of pain for a few different types of headaches.

- **Sinus headaches.** Sinuses are hollow spaces in your head. You have four sets of sinuses: two behind your nose, two in your cheekbones, two in your forehead, and two in your brain, behind your nasal passages. If any of these sinuses get congested or inflamed, it can cause pain. Colds, infections, and allergies are common causes of sinus headaches.

Text-Dependent Questions

1. What happens in the brain during an epileptic seizure?
2. What are the two categories of epileptic seizure? What is the difference between them?
3. Name three different types of headaches. Which types are generally the most painful? Which type is caused by stress?

Research Project

What would you do if you were babysitting some younger kids, and one of them had a seizure? This guide from the Epilepsy Foundation tells you exactly what to do: www.epilepsy.com/learn/seizures-youth/childcare-professionals-and-babysitters-guide/babysitters-guide-first-aid. Read it, and write up your own list of safety tips.

WORDS TO UNDERSTAND

atypical: different from most.

dementia: brain disorders that destroy the ability to think, reason, or remember.

***de novo* mutations:** genetic mutation caused by random errors in DNA.

electrolytes: ions that circulate in blood and tissues.

epileptologist: a doctor who specializes in treating epilepsy.

hallucinate: to see, hear, or otherwise sense something that isn't actually there.

sclerosis: when normally soft body tissues become hard.

status epilepticus: severe epileptic seizures lasting five or more minutes, or occurring in rapid succession.

syndrome: a condition with a set of associated symptoms.

CHAPTER THREE

Epilepsy

You may think of epilepsy as a single disease. But it's actually a catch-all term for any disease or **syndrome** that causes electrochemical seizures. If you have had two or more electrochemical seizures, you have epilepsy. One important exception is when seizures are caused by a temporary condition, like a high fever, an infection, a traumatic brain injury, or very high or very low levels of blood sugar or **electrolytes**. But if a person continues to suffer from seizures after the end of that temporary condition, that person is diagnosed with epilepsy.

Neurologists and **epileptologists**—doctors who specialize in caring for people with epilepsy and seizure disorders—use the term "the epilepsies" to better describe how many different syndromes and conditions cause epileptic seizures.

The epilepsies are more common than you might think. Nearly 3 million Americans have an epilepsy diagnosis. Half a million kids and teenagers have epilepsy. In fact, the epilepsies are more common among children and the elderly. Kids with epilepsy may grow out of it, depending on the condition that caused it. In older people, epilepsy is generally the result of

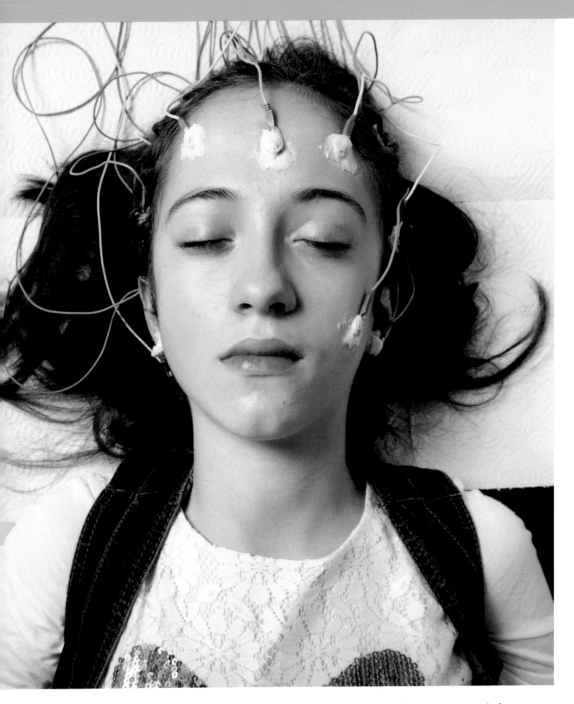

If it is suspected that someone has some form of epilepsy, doctors may ask for an electroencephalogram (EEG), which uses electrodes to monitor electrical activity in the brain.

injuries to the brain that are associated with aging. Strokes and different forms of **dementia**, particularly Alzheimer's disease, can damage the brain's ability to send and receive signals.

Kids and the Epilepsies

In children, the epilepsies are generally caused by genetic mutations. Genetic mutations occur when the instructions in your DNA telling your cells how to develop get garbled or even deleted. Scientists are still learning which parts of those instructions affect the development of epilepsy. Some of the mutations that cause epilepsy are known. But many remain unknown. In up to half of epilepsy cases, doctors do not know the cause at all. Scientists believe there are likely to be hundreds of different genetic mutations that may affect a person's susceptibility to epilepsy. Most of these mutations are still undiscovered.

There are two broad types of genetic mutations. Some mutations occur spontaneously. Called *de novo* **mutations**, these may happen by random chance. Other genetic mutations are inherited—that is, they are passed down from parent to child. Some epilepsy syndromes run in families. These are linked to inherited mutations. Other epilepsy syndromes do not seem to run in families, and are probably a result of *de novo* mutations.

Kids and teens may also develop epilepsy due to damage done to the brain by a traumatic brain injury. Car crashes, bike crashes, certain sports injuries, concussions, and gunshot wounds are some of the common causes of traumatic brain injuries. Meningitis, an infection of the meninges that protects the brain and spinal cord, may also cause epilepsy.

Epilepsy Syndromes

Scientists know of hundreds of different epilepsy syndromes. Let's take a closer look at some of the most common.

STATUS EPILEPTICUS

Status epilepticus is a very serious condition in which seizures may not stop on their own. Someone in status epilepticus needs emergency medical treatment to stop the seizures. Without help, the person may suffer injuries, brain damage, even death.

These conditions define status epilepticus:

- A seizure that lasts for five minutes or longer.
- Two or more seizures occurring so close together that the person cannot recover or regain consciousness between them.
- Multiple seizures occurring within 30 minutes.

Status epilepticus can happen during convulsive seizures, like tonic-clonic seizures. It can also happen during nonconvulsive seizures, like absence seizures. Nonconvulsive status epilepticus can be tricky to spot. But if someone remains confused, distant, or incoherent for more than five minutes, it may be status epilepticus. Status epilepticus is very rare. But if you or someone you love has a history of seizures, it's important to have a seizure emergency plan so that everyone knows what to do, just in case.

Temporal Lobe Epilepsy. This is the most common form of epilepsy, accounting for nearly 60 percent of epilepsy diagnoses. These focal seizures occur in one of the brain's temporal lobes, but can spread to both sides of the brain. If you have temporal lobe epilepsy, you may have weird or intense feelings either before or during a seizure. You may suddenly feel scared, angry, or joyful for no reason. You may hallucinate, seeing, hearing, or smelling things that aren't really there. You may have simple seizures, in which you remain aware of what's going on during the seizure. You may have complex seizures, in which you lose awareness or consciousness of what is happening. You may have automatisms or jerking. You may speak gibberish, or lose the ability to speak during the seizure.

Medication controls the seizures for about two-thirds of people. The remaining third may find some relief from surgery, particularly if part of the temporal lobe shows signs of abnormal hardening, or **sclerosis**, in brain scans. Some people with temporal lobe epilepsy may also use a vagus nerve implant to help control seizures.

Juvenile Myoclonic Epilepsy. Another common epilepsy syndrome, this one has genetic causes and runs in families. It usually begins between the ages of 5 and 16 with absence seizures. Later, myoclonic (jerking) seizures and tonic-clonic seizures develop. Seizures are associated with waking up. They are more likely to occur when a person is sleep-deprived or stressed, and they are made worse by drinking alcohol. Avoiding these triggers and being careful to take prescribed anti-seizure medications can help reduce the risk of seizures.

Benign Rolandic Epilepsy. Affecting up to 15 percent of kids with epilepsy, this syndrome usually causes simple focal seizures that sometimes develop into tonic seizures. These seizures are generally infrequent. Many kids with benign rolandic epilepsy grow out of it and stop having seizures altogether by around age 16.

Childhood Absence Epilepsy. This syndrome causes very brief absence seizures lasting 10 to 20 seconds at a time. The child is unconscious during the seizure, staring blankly into space. People with childhood absence epilepsy

EDUCATIONAL VIDEO

Scan this code to watch a video about a teenage girl with juvenile myoclonic epilepsy.

may blink rapidly or roll their eyes. Because this syndrome can cause over a hundred such seizures in a single day, it can make it hard for kids to learn or do well in school.

But in two-thirds of cases, this syndrome responds well to medication. The majority of kids with childhood absence epilepsy grow out of it, but kids with a similar syndrome called *juvenile absence epilepsy* may have to take medication to control seizures for their whole lives. Both syndromes have genetic causes.

Frontal Lobe Epilepsy. This syndrome can be caused by a number of things, including genetics and brain injuries. When a seizure occurs in a frontal lobe, a person's arms and legs may jerk violently. The person sometimes shrieks, giggles, or grimaces. If the seizure spreads to both sides of the brain, tonic-clonic seizures occur. Frontal lobe epilepsy can be treated with medications, surgery to the affected lobe, or a vagus nerve implant.

Reflex Epilepsies. This is a group of syndromes that cause people to develop seizures, usually tonic-clonic, in response to a certain stimulus. Flashing

 EPILEPSY AND AUTISM

Autism is a developmental disability. Someone with autism has unusual or **atypical** networks and pathways in his or her brain. This can cause difficulty with speech and nonverbal communication. People with autism often have trouble in social situations. Autism can also affect how the brain processes information from the senses.

People with autism are much more likely to have epilepsy than people without autism. Up to one in three people with autism develop seizures. People with both autism and intellectual disabilities are at very high risk for epilepsy. Scientists are still trying to determine why that might be.

Flickering fluorescent bulbs are one potential cause of seizures for people with reflex epilepsy.

lights are the most common stimulus. These can be anything from flickering fluorescent light bulbs to video games, TV shows, or even patterns of light and shade under a tree on a windy day. Reflex epilepsies run in families. Kids may outgrow their seizures, but it's important to continue taking anti-seizure medications unless a doctor instructs you to stop.

Dravet Syndrome. This very serious syndrome is caused by a *de novo* genetic mutation that affects the way the brain uses ions to create electrochemical messages. First seizures may develop in infancy and may be of almost any type.

SUDDEN UNEXPLAINED DEATH IN EPILEPSY

The most tragic complication of epilepsy goes by the acronym SUDEP, for Sudden Unexplained Death in Epilepsy. It is very rare in children and teenagers. But it is the most common cause of death in adults ages 20–40 with uncontrolled seizures. It is less common in people who have only absence or myoclonic seizures. SUDEP is more likely in people who have both intellectual disabilities and epilepsy.

Doctors do not know what causes SUDEP. It may occur while the person is sleeping. In about a third of cases, there is clear evidence that the person had a seizure before dying. Until scientists have a better understanding of what causes SUDEP, the best way to prevent it is to take your medication as directed. If your seizures are under control, your risk of SUDEP is very, very small.

People with Dravet syndrome sometimes suffer from lengthy, life-threatening seizures called **status epilepticus** (see sidebar on p. 40). Seizures can be triggered by a long list of causes, including fever or other infection, stress, excitement, flashing lights, and even warm baths. Kids with Dravet syndrome generally have developmental disabilities that affect behavior and thinking, including autism.

Infantile Spasms. A rare syndrome, this causes babies to jerk and stiffen, often just as they are waking up or falling asleep. While these seizures generally end by the time the child is four years old, kids who had infantile spasms often go on to develop another epilepsy syndrome. They are also more likely to have intellectual disabilities, or developmental disabilities like autism.

Lennox-Gastaut Syndrome. Poorly understood and very difficult to treat, this rare syndrome usually begins in early childhood, and, unlike many types of epilepsy, it is a lifelong condition. It affects more boys than girls, and is more common in kids who had infantile spasms. Most people with this syndrome have intellectual disabilities, often severe enough to prevent them from living on their own as adults. A ketogenic diet may help control seizures in cases where medications do not.

Rett Syndrome. A genetic disorder that happens only to girls, Rett syndrome affects brain development in many different ways, including the ability to speak, move muscles, and control behavior. It also causes epileptic seizures. There is no cure for Rett syndrome, though women who have it may live to their 40s or 50s despite their poor health.

Text-Dependent Questions

1. What are two types of genetic mutations that might cause a kid to develop one of the epilepsies?
2. Which epilepsy syndrome can cause up to a hundred absence seizures per day?
3. Which epilepsy syndrome is the most common?

Research Project

A national campaign called talkaboutit.org makes short videos urging people to learn more about seizures and epilepsy. Look around the website and watch some of the group's videos. What would you want other people to know about epilepsy? Write your own script or PSA.

WORDS TO UNDERSTAND

discrimination: when a person is treated unequally or unjustly because of some condition (health status, race, gender, etc.).

prejudice: hateful or hostile discrimination.

stigma: shame or disgrace.

transcranial: passing through the skull.

CHAPTER FOUR

The Past, Present, and Future of Epilepsy

Epilepsy is one of the oldest known human illnesses. It appears in the historical record as far back as Hammurabi's Code, a set of laws written in ancient Mesopotamia in 1754 BCE. These laws stated that a person with epilepsy was not allowed to get married or testify in court. It may seem hard to believe, but people with epilepsy have faced crippling legal **discrimination** and social **prejudice** for thousands of years. Even in the United States, laws once forbade people with epilepsy from getting married. Laws also allowed restaurants, theaters, and other places to deny service to people with epilepsy. The last of these laws was repealed only in 1980—well within the lifetimes of your parents and grandparents.

The basis for this discrimination and prejudice was the ancient idea that epilepsy was a sort of divine curse, a punishment sent by the gods. The famous Greek physician Hippocrates argued against this belief as early as 400 BCE. But the belief persisted, and was adopted by early Christians, who taught that people with epilepsy were possessed by demons. They also taught that epilepsy was

The Code of Hammurabi from around 1750 BCE admonished that people with what we now call epilepsy should not be allowed to marry.

TELEVISION-INDUCED SEIZURES

In 1997, Japanese kids loved a new TV show about fierce, adorable pocket monsters, called Pokémon. But one episode became a worldwide scandal. Over four million children were watching the cartoon when a short burst of rapidly flashing red and blue lights provoked seizures in some viewers. Six hundred and eighty-five people called ambulances, and about 150 kids were admitted to hospitals because of these seizures. Only a small percentage of those hospitalized were eventually diagnosed with epilepsy. But the television show was pulled off the air for four months while researchers determined exactly what caused so many people to have seizures all at once. Animators changed their techniques to ensure such a thing never happened again.

contagious. Today we know these ideas were all wrong. But until very recently, the **stigma** caused by these beliefs made life very difficult for people with epilepsy.

Our laws have changed for the better, but the stigma still persists in some subtle ways. Sometimes kids with epilepsy and other seizure disorders get bullied or lose friends because of their seizures. If you have seizures, you may feel a lot of anxiety about what other people may think or do if you have a seizure in public. The good news is that teaching people the facts about epilepsy and seizures really makes a difference. The more people know about epilepsy, the less likely they are to hold negative beliefs and prejudices about it. And the more you know about epilepsy, the more you can do to help keep someone safe during a seizure.

Epilepsy at Home

If you've been diagnosed with epilepsy, your neurologist or epileptologist is a vital part of the team that helps you prevent and treat seizures. You and your family are the most important members of that team. With advice from your doctor and other medical professionals, your family will set up a treatment plan. If you are prescribed medications to prevent or control your seizures, take those medications according to your doctor's directions. It's important to get in the habit of taking your medications without fail. Missing a dose of medication can trigger seizures.

Getting enough sleep is a key part of controlling epilepsy. Unfortunately, our electronic devices tend to keep us awake; you are better off keeping your phone and tablet out of your bedroom.

Some anti-seizure medications produce side effects. If you are bothered by side effects, make a note of your experiences so that you can discuss them with your doctor. Your medical team may be able to adjust your medications to reduce side effects.

EDUCATIONAL VIDEO

Scan this code to watch a video about teenagers and epilepsy.

Sleep deprivation is a common trigger of seizures. It's hard sometimes to find the time and the willpower to get yourself to bed, especially when you're busy or having fun. But getting enough sleep is one of the best ways to take care of yourself.

Your medical team will offer safety tips and precautions to minimize your risk if you do have a seizure. The specifics will vary, depending on the kinds of seizures you have and how frequently they occur. For example, you may be advised to stay off high places from which you might fall during a seizure. You may be advised to use a buddy system in certain situations. Many doctors advise swimming or riding a bike only when you are with someone who could help if you have a seizure. Because it is possible to drown in only an inch or two of water, you may be told to take showers instead of baths. In some cases, doctors recommend that you shower only when someone else is home with you. Leave the bathroom door unlocked so that someone can reach you quickly in case of emergency.

It's important that everyone you live with knows what to do if you have a seizure. Keep a list of instructions and emergency numbers posted in a place where everyone can see it.

Showers may be safer than baths for people with epilepsy. Talk to your doctor about whether showers or baths are best for you.

Epilepsy at School

At school you might be worried about more than just your safety if you have a seizure. You may feel anxious or embarrassed about what other kids will think. Epilepsy isn't contagious, and it isn't your fault if you have epilepsy. But it can be hard when you feel different from other kids. You may struggle with low self-esteem or feel bad about yourself. It's good to have somebody you can talk to who will really understand how epilepsy affects your life. Your doctor may be

FAMOUS PEOPLE WITH EPILEPSY

Seizures couldn't stop these famous people from achieving their dreams in life.

- **John Roberts.** The chief justice of the United States Supreme Court had his first seizure as an adult, in 1993. His second seizure, in 2007, caused him to fall from a height, but did not result in serious injury.
- **Fyodor Dostoyevsky.** This 19th century Russian novelist is considered one of the greatest writers of all time. He had temporal lobe seizures. He kept written records of 102 seizures he experienced between 1860 and his death in 1881. He also wrote vivid descriptions of seizures in his novels, some of which featured epileptic characters.
- **Prince.** The groundbreaking, best-selling rock musician had seizures as a child. In a 2009 interview, he told the journalist Tavis Smiley that his epilepsy was one of the challenges that inspired him to become "as flashy as I could, and as noisy as I could."

WHEN SOMEONE IS HAVING A SEIZURE

These are the steps for putting someone in what is called "the recovery position." This position helps keep the person's airway open so that they can breathe easily.

In most cases, a seizure lasts less than a minute. If you're with a person having a seizure, chances are you won't need to do anything except wait until it's over. Then you can ask if the person is okay or needs anything.

Someone having tonic-clonic seizures, with convulsions and falls, may need your help to stay safe. Here's what doctors recommend if you're with someone having a severe seizure:

- Move anything hard or sharp away from the person that could cause injury.
- If you can, put a jacket or pillow under the person's head.
- Turn the person onto one side. This can prevent choking.
- If there is anything around the person's neck, make sure it's loose and doesn't restrict breathing.
- Don't try to hold the person down or stop any movements.
- Don't put anything in the person's mouth.

If the person is injured during the seizure, make sure to stay nearby until proper medical attention is provided. If the person has trouble breathing, or seizures last five minutes or longer, emergency medical help is needed. The best thing to do in an emergency is call 911.

able to direct you to counselors or support groups for kids, teens, and families dealing with epilepsy in your area.

Support groups can give you good advice about how to handle issues that come up with your friends and at school. If you can't find anything in your area, check out the website of the Epilepsy Foundation (www.epilepsy.com); they even have a weekly moderated chat where you can ask questions. No matter where you find support, always remember that you're not alone. Of the nearly half a million American children who have epilepsy, at least 300,000 are in school right now. That's a lot of kids who know what you're going through.

If your seizures make it difficult to learn, you may qualify for certain special education services under the Individuals with Disabilities Education Act (IDEA). Your family can push for an evaluation that determines what your school can do to help you get the most out of your education. School staff members will need to know what to do if you have a seizure at school. The school nurse, your teachers, even your school bus driver should be aware of your situation and have clear instructions about how to help you if you have a seizure.

The Future of Epilepsy

Many types of epilepsy get better as a child gets older. And many kids find that medication controls their seizures quite well. But there is always more that could be done. That's why current research on epilepsy is looking at several different ways to improve life for people with seizures.

First, researchers are looking to understand more about the causes of epilepsy. Some genetic causes are known, but many others are yet to be found. Scientists hope that knowing more about what can cause epileptic seizures may allow us to one day prevent seizures from developing in the first place.

Second, doctors and researchers are trying to find new and improved drugs that can control seizures better while causing fewer side effects. They particularly want to find medications that will work on refractory seizures, those seizures that do not respond to currently available treatments.

Finally, there is a lot of scientific interest and excitement about the possibility of better and more advanced electric implants that can monitor focal areas of the brain for signs of seizure activity and tamp it down before it even begins. Another experimental treatment that shows promise is **transcranial** magnetic stimulation, which uses magnets to affect the brain's tendency to develop abnormal signals.

If you or someone you care about has seizures, all of these research directions are good reasons to have hope for the future. While epileptic seizures can place some limits on what you can do, they can't stop you from making the most of your life.

Text-Dependent Questions

1. In what ways have people with epilepsy faced discrimination throughout history?
2. What are two important ways to take care of yourself if you have epilepsy?
3. Name one way that scientists are trying to help people with epilepsy.

Research Project

An essay by Joyce Cramer argues that people with epilepsy need new ways to make sure they don't forget to take their medications. The essay is available on the website of the Epilepsy Foundation, at www.epilepsy.com/article/2014/3/titanic-impact-medication-compliance-epilepsy. Read the essay, and then think of three ways to help someone take their medications every day.

FURTHER READING

Christopherson, Sara Cohen. *Living with Epilepsy.* Living With Health Challenges. Minneapolis, MN: ABDO, 2012.

Epilepsy Foundation. www.epilepsy.com.

Gay, Kathlyn, and Sean McGarrahan. *Epilepsy: The Ultimate Teen Guide.* Lanham, MD: Scarecrow Press, 2007.

Mayo Clinic Staff. "Migraine: Overview." Rochester, MN: Mayo Clinic. http://www.mayoclinic.org/diseases-conditions/migraine-headache/home/ovc-20202432.

TeensHealth. "Migraine Headaches." http://kidshealth.org/en/teens/migraines.html.

Wilner, Andrew. *Epilepsy: 199 Answers: A Doctor Responds to His Patients' Questions.* New York: Demos Health, 2008.

Wyllie, Elaine. *Cleveland Clinic Guide to Epilepsy: Essential Reading for Families.* 3rd ed. New York: Kaplan, 2016.

Young, William B., and Stephen D. Silberstein. *Migraine and Other Headaches.* New York: Demos Health, 2004.

Educational Videos

Chapter One: KidsHealth.org. "Nervous System." https://youtu.be/dah-4mtAnsQ.

Chapter Two: British Red Cross. "Children First Aid: Seizure." https://youtu.be/vSnRdmR6xcE.

Chapter Three: Jenn Jenn. "Epilepsy and Me." https://youtu.be/Pa1wWCzhoiI.

Chapter Four: Pscribner. "Out of the Shadows: Teens with Epilepsy Take Charge." https://youtu.be/0sN2fyeJ-hY.

SERIES GLOSSARY

accommodation: an arrangement or adjustment to a new situation; for example, schools make accommodations to help students cope with illness.

anemia: an illness caused by a lack of red blood cells.

autoimmune: type of disorder where the body's immune system attacks the body's tissues instead of germs.

benign: not harmful.

biofeedback: a technique used to teach someone how to control some bodily functions.

capillaries: tiny blood vessels that carry blood from larger blood vessels to body tissues.

carcinogens: substances that can cause cancer to develop.

cerebellum: the back part of the brain; it controls movement.

cerebrum: the front part of the brain; it controls many higher-level thinking and functions.

cholesterol: a waxy substance associated with fats that coats the inside of blood vessels, causing cardiovascular disease.

cognitive: related to conscious mental activities, such as learning and thinking.

communicable: transferable from one person to another.

congenital: a condition or disorder that exists from birth.

correlation: a connection between different things that suggests they may have something to do with one another.

dominant: in genetics, a dominant trait is expressed in a child even when the trait is only inherited from one parent.

environmental factors: anything that affects how people live, develop, or grow. Climate, diet, and pollution are examples.

genes: units of hereditary information.

hemorrhage: bleeding from a broken blood vessel.

hormones: substances the body produces to instruct cells and tissues to perform certain actions.

inflammation: redness, swelling, and tenderness in a part of the body in response to infection or injury.

insulin: a hormone produced in the pancreas that controls cells' ability to absorb glucose.

lymphatic system: part of the human immune system; transports white blood cells around the body.

malignant: harmful; relating to tumors, likely to spread.

mutation: a change in the structure of a gene; some mutations are harmless, but others may cause disease.

neurological: relating to the nervous system (including the brain and spinal cord).

neurons: specialized cells found in the central nervous system (the brain and spinal cord).

occupational therapy: a type of therapy that teaches one how to accomplish tasks and activities in daily life.

oncology: the study of cancer.

orthopedic: dealing with deformities in bones or muscles.

prevalence: how common or uncommon a disease is in any given population.

prognosis: the forecast for the course of a disease that predicts whether a person with the disease will get sicker, recover, or stay the same.

progressive disease: a disease that generally gets worse as time goes on.

psychomotor: relating to movement or muscle activity resulting from mental activity.

recessive: in genetics, a recessive trait will only be expressed if a child inherits it from both parents.

remission: an improvement in or disappearance of someone's symptoms of disease; unlike a cure, remission is usually temporary.

resilience: the ability to bounce back from difficult situations.

seizure: an event caused by unusual brain activity resulting in physical or behavior changes.

syndrome: a condition with a set of associated symptoms.

ulcers: a break or sore in skin or tissue where cells disintegrate and die. Infections may occur at the site of an ulcer.

INDEX

Illlustrations are indicated by page numbers in *italic* type.

ABOUT THE ADVISOR

Heather Pelletier, Ph.D., is a pediatric staff psychologist at Rhode Island Hospital/Hasbro Children's Hospital with a joint appointment as a clinical assistant professor in the departments of Psychiatry and Human Behavior and Pediatrics at the Warren Alpert Medical School of Brown University. She is also the director of behavioral pain medicine in the division of Children's Integrative therapies, Pain management and Supportive care (CHIPS) in the department of Pediatrics at Hasbro Children's Hospital. Dr. Pelletier provides clinical services to children in various medical specialty clinics at Hasbro Children's Hospital, including the pediatric gastroenterology, nutrition, and liver disease clinics.

ABOUT THE AUTHOR

Rebecca Sherman writes about health care policy, public health issues, and parenting. She lives in Massachusetts with her family.

PHOTO CREDITS